Green Living on a Budget

A Guide to Sustainable Eating and Healthy Living

Carla Windsor

Table of Contents

Introduction — 5

Chapter 1 — 9

Understanding Green Living — 9

    What is Green Living? — 9

    Why Green Living Matters — 13

    The Benefits of Green Living — 17

Chapter 2 — 21

Living Sustainably on a Budget — 21

    Setting Your Green Living Goals — 21

    Creating a Green Living Budget — 25

    Eco-Friendly Lifestyle Hacks — 29

Chapter 3 — 35

The Importance of Sustainable Eating — 35

    Food and Environmental Impact — 35

    The Ethics of Food Choices — 40

    Sustainable Eating Benefits — 45

Chapter 4 — 49

Budget-Friendly Green Eating — 49

    Smart Grocery Shopping — 49

    Meal Planning for Sustainability — 54

    Reducing Food Waste — 58

Chapter 5 — 63

Green Kitchen Practices — 63

    Energy-Efficient Cooking — 63

Reducing Plastic in the Kitchen   68

Growing Your Own Food   73

Chapter 6   **77**

Holistic Health and Green Living   **77**

Connecting Your Health to the Environment   77

Eco-Friendly Personal Care   82

Exercise and Sustainable Living   86

Chapter 7   **89**

Green Home and Cleaning   **89**

Non-Toxic Cleaning Products   89

Creating a Healthy Home Environment   94

Energy-Efficient Living   99

Chapter 8   **105**

Advocating for Green Living   **105**

Spreading the Word   105

Supporting Sustainable Initiatives   110

Engaging with Your Community   115

Conclusion   **121**

Introduction

Have you ever walked through a bustling supermarket, filled with endless aisles of colorful packaging, and wondered about the true cost of the food on your plate? Or perhaps you've looked around your home, realizing just how many items are made from synthetic materials that could be harming your health and the planet? If you've ever felt that pang of concern, that desire to make a change, you're not alone. The world is awakening to the need for a more sustainable and healthier way of living, and it starts with you.

In the pages of this book, "Green Living on a Budget: A Guide to Sustainable Eating and Healthy Living," we embark on a journey of discovery and transformation. We will explore how you can embrace a greener, more environmentally responsible way of life without emptying your wallet, and, more importantly, how you can nourish your body and the Earth in the process.

But why should you care about green living? Because, in this age of rapid change and mounting environmental challenges, it's not just a trend; it's a powerful movement driven by a desire for a better, more sustainable future. It's about leaving a legacy that our children and grandchildren can be proud of.

Imagine waking up each day with a sense of purpose, knowing that your choices are contributing to a healthier planet, and ultimately, a healthier you. Picture a life where you savor each meal, knowing that the food you eat is not only delicious but also produced with respect for the environment. Envision a home that feels like a sanctuary, where every product and material inside it is carefully chosen to support your well-being and reduce your ecological footprint.

As you read these pages, you'll discover practical, budget-friendly strategies for sustainable eating, eco-friendly living, and cultivating a sense of well-being that extends far beyond yourself. But more than that, you'll tap into an emotional connection, a powerful yearning to be a part of something greater. We'll explore how you can make choices that align with your values and, in doing so, become a vital force in the global movement toward a greener, healthier world.

So, whether you're driven by the desire to protect our beautiful planet, improve your health, save money, or simply feel more connected to your purpose in life, this book is your guide. The journey starts here, and it's a journey you won't want to miss.

Are you ready to make a profound difference in your life and the world? Let's take the first step together, and as we do, be prepared to be inspired, empowered, and deeply moved. It's time to embrace a greener, healthier life.

But why should you care about green living?

It's about leaving a legacy that our children and grandchildren can be proud of.

Chapter 1

Understanding Green Living

What is Green Living?

In this chapter, we're diving headfirst into the world of green living. What is it, you ask? Well, let's unravel the mysteries and myths, shall we?

What is Green Living?

Green living, my friends, is like a cool breeze on a hot summer day for our planet. It's all about living in a way that minimizes harm to the environment and prioritizes sustainability. Think of it as a lifestyle that fosters harmony between you and Mother Earth. It's not about giving up your comforts or living like a hermit in the woods; it's about making conscious choices that reduce your ecological footprint and promote a healthier, more sustainable world.

The Three Pillars of Green Living

1. Environmental Responsibility: This is all about reducing your impact on the planet. It's choosing to bike instead of drive, composting your kitchen scraps, or using energy-efficient appliances. Small changes that, collectively, make a massive difference.

2. Economic Efficiency: Green living isn't just about hugging trees; it's also about watching your wallet. It means being savvy with your resources, finding budget-friendly ways to reduce waste, and making choices that save you money in the long run. Who doesn't love a win-win?

3. Healthy Living: The cherry on top is that green living often leads to a healthier, happier you. By choosing organic, locally sourced foods and reducing your exposure to harmful chemicals, you're not just saving the planet but also investing in your well-being.

The Green Living Misconceptions

Now, here's where things get interesting. There are a few misconceptions about green living that need debunking.

Misconception 1: It's Too Expensive

This one's a classic, right? The belief that sustainable choices will drain your bank account. Well, it's time to bust that myth. Sure, some eco-products can be pricey, but that doesn't mean you have to buy them all. We'll explore budget-friendly options, DIY solutions, and smart choices that won't break the bank.

Misconception 2: It's Inconvenient

Green living is often seen as a hassle. Who wants to go out of their way to save the environment? But the truth is, it's not all that inconvenient. In fact, we'll show you how it can make life easier. No more last-minute runs to the store, no more wasting time and resources on things you don't need.

Misconception 3: It Doesn't Make a Difference

You might think, "I'm just one person. Can I really make a change?" Oh, but you can! We'll tell you stories of individuals who started small and created a ripple effect. Your actions matter, and we'll prove it.

The Journey Ahead

So, dear reader, welcome to the world of green living. Over the course of this book, we'll navigate through the complexities and simplify the process. You'll discover practical tips, real-life stories, and a roadmap to start your green living journey. The road may have a few bumps, but together, we'll make it a smooth ride. Get ready to embrace a lifestyle that's not just eco-friendly but wallet-friendly and body-friendly too. Green living is not a trend; it's a way of life, and it's time you joined the club!

Why Green Living Matters

Green living is not just a fad or a niche interest for tree-huggers and activists; it's a lifestyle that matters profoundly in today's world. Let's delve into the reasons why embracing green living is crucial for our planet, our health, and our future.

1. Environmental Preservation

At the heart of green living is the preservation of our environment. Our planet faces unprecedented challenges, from climate change to deforestation, pollution, and the depletion of natural resources. These issues are not just statistics; they impact the air we breathe, the water we drink, and the future we leave for our children. Green living is a commitment to reducing our ecological footprint and protecting the delicate balance of our ecosystems. It's about safeguarding the beauty and diversity of our world.

2. Mitigating Climate Change

Climate change is one of the most urgent and critical global challenges we face. The burning of fossil fuels, deforestation, and industrial processes release greenhouse gases into the atmosphere, trapping heat and causing global temperatures to rise. Green living encourages practices such as reducing energy consumption, supporting renewable energy sources, and minimizing waste, all of which contribute to reducing our carbon footprint. Each small action collectively makes a big impact in the fight against climate change.

3. Resource Conservation

Our planet's resources are finite, and many are being depleted at an alarming rate. Green living promotes responsible resource management, from conserving water and energy to reducing waste and using sustainable materials. By making the most of what we have and reusing or recycling when possible, we can ensure a more sustainable future for generations to come.

4. Health and Well-being

Green living isn't just about saving the planet; it's about improving our health and well-being. By choosing eco-friendly products, eating organic, and reducing exposure to harmful chemicals, we can lead healthier lives. The air we breathe, the food we eat, and the products we use all impact our health. Green living empowers us to make choices that support our long-term well-being.

5. Economic Savings

Contrary to the misconception that green living is expensive, it can save you money in the long run. Energy-efficient appliances, reduced water usage, and less waste mean lower utility bills. Additionally, sustainable practices like growing your food or buying locally can result in cost savings. Green living isn't just about protecting the environment; it's also about protecting your wallet.

6. Global Responsibility

We are part of a global community, and our choices have far-reaching effects. By adopting green living practices, we acknowledge our role in the interconnected web of life on Earth. We recognize that our actions impact not only our local community but also people and ecosystems across the globe. Green living is a commitment to being responsible global citizens.

7. Setting an Example

Leading by example is a powerful way to inspire others. When we embrace green living, we influence our friends, family, and community to do the same. Our choices can create a domino effect of positive change, contributing to a collective shift toward a more sustainable and harmonious world.

In conclusion, green living matters because it's about more than just our immediate surroundings; it's about the legacy we leave for future generations. It's about our planet's health, our well-being, and our global responsibility. It's a commitment to making a difference, no matter how small our actions may seem. Together, through green living, we can work towards a brighter, more sustainable future for all.

The Benefits of Green Living

Green living isn't just about reducing your environmental impact; it comes with a host of tangible and intangible benefits that can enhance your life in various ways. Let's explore the numerous advantages of embracing a greener lifestyle:

1. Environmental Stewardship

First and foremost, green living allows you to become a responsible steward of the environment. By adopting sustainable practices, you reduce your carbon footprint, conserve natural resources, and help protect the planet's ecosystems. Your actions contribute to the preservation of Earth's beauty and diversity.

2. Improved Health

Green living often goes hand in hand with healthier living. Choosing organic, locally sourced foods and reducing exposure to harmful chemicals can lead to improved personal health. Additionally, walking or biking instead of driving and embracing a more active lifestyle can boost physical well-being.

3. Cost Savings

Contrary to the misconception that eco-friendly choices are expensive, green living can save you money. Energy-efficient appliances, reduced water consumption, and less waste result in lower utility bills. Growing your food or supporting local markets can also lead to cost savings.

4. Cleaner Air and Water

Reducing air pollution and minimizing the use of harmful chemicals in your home and garden can lead to cleaner air and water in your surroundings. This contributes to a healthier environment for you and your community.

5. Reduced Stress

Living in harmony with nature and simplifying your life by decluttering and minimizing waste can lead to reduced stress. A cleaner, more organized living space can promote a sense of peace and well-being.

6. Stronger Community Bonds

Engaging in green living practices often means connecting with your local community. Joining community gardens, participating in environmental initiatives, and supporting local businesses can foster a sense of belonging and community engagement.

7. Self-Sufficiency

Growing your food or generating renewable energy, like solar power, can make you more self-sufficient. It reduces your dependence on external sources and empowers you to take control of your resources.

8. Positive Impact on Future Generations

Green living isn't just about the present; it's about the future. By adopting sustainable practices, you leave a positive legacy for your children and future generations. You pave the way for a more sustainable and equitable world.

9. Increased Awareness and Mindfulness

Green living encourages you to be more mindful of your choices. You become aware of the environmental impact of your decisions, leading to a greater sense of responsibility and consciousness in your daily life.

10. Inspiration and Empowerment

By embracing green living, you can inspire others and empower them to make positive changes in their lives. Your actions can create a ripple effect of awareness and action, contributing to a larger movement for positive change.

In conclusion, green living isn't just about saving the planet; it's about enhancing the quality of your life in numerous ways. It's a holistic approach that addresses environmental, personal, and community well-being. By adopting sustainable practices, you can lead a more fulfilling and purposeful life while contributing to a better, greener world for all.

Chapter 2

Living Sustainably on a Budget

Setting Your Green Living Goals

Alright, so you're ready to embrace green living, but you're concerned about the costs, right? Chapter 2's got your back. Here, we'll explore how to live sustainably without breaking the bank. It all starts with setting your green living goals.

Setting Your Green Living Goals

First things first, let's set the stage. Setting clear, achievable goals is the secret sauce to success in green living on a budget. Why? Because it gives you direction, and a roadmap to follow.

1. Define Your Priorities

What matters most to you? Is it reducing waste, using renewable energy, or eating sustainably? List your priorities. Maybe you want to focus on energy conservation or start composting. Having a few key goals helps you channel your efforts effectively.

2. Make SMART Goals

You've probably heard of SMART goals, Specific, Measurable, Achievable, Relevant, and Time-bound. Let's break it down:

Specific: Be clear and precise about what you want to achieve. For instance, "Reduce household energy consumption by 15% within six months."

Measurable: Define how you'll measure success. Whether it's tracking your energy usage or the amount of waste you generate, have a way to measure your progress.

Achievable: Set goals that are within your reach. Don't aim to completely overhaul your lifestyle overnight; start with manageable steps.

Relevant: Ensure your goals align with your values and make a real impact on your green living journey.

Time-bound: Establish a timeline for your goals. It could be weekly, monthly, or even annually. Deadlines keep you accountable.

3. Create an Action Plan

Now that you have your goals, let's create a plan to achieve them. Break down your goals into smaller, actionable steps. For instance, if your goal is to reduce household waste, your action steps might include starting a compost bin, using reusable shopping bags, and buying products with minimal packaging.

4. Stay Flexible and Learn

Life happens, and sometimes plans need adjusting. Stay flexible and open to learning. Not every method will work perfectly the first time, and that's okay. Adjust, learn, and keep moving forward.

5. Celebrate Your Wins

Remember to celebrate your achievements, no matter how small. Did you manage to cut your electricity bill by 5%? High five! Celebrating your wins keeps you motivated and engaged in your green living journey.

Final Thoughts

Your green living goals aren't just a checklist; they're a guiding light, a way to steer your lifestyle toward a more sustainable path. As you set your goals, remember it's a journey, not a race. Embrace the progress and the lessons along the way. Your commitment to living sustainably on a budget starts with these goals, paving the way for a greener, more fulfilling life.

Creating a Green Living Budget

Living sustainably doesn't have to mean breaking the bank. It can often save you money in the long run. In this section, we'll explore how to create a green living budget that aligns with your eco-friendly goals and financial well-being.

1. Assess Your Current Spending

The first step to creating a green living budget is to understand where your money is going. Take a close look at your current spending habits. How much are you spending on utilities, transportation, food, and other expenses? This assessment will help you identify areas where you can make eco-friendly and budget-conscious changes.

2. Prioritize Green Choices

Now that you have a clear view of your spending, identify areas where you can prioritize green choices. *For example:*

Energy Efficiency: Look for ways to reduce your energy consumption, such as switching to LED bulbs, sealing drafts, and using energy-efficient appliances.

Reduce, Reuse, Recycle: Embrace the 3 R's. Reduce waste by buying products with minimal packaging, reuse items whenever possible, and recycle to keep materials out of landfills.

Sustainable Transportation: Consider walking, biking, carpooling, or using public transportation to reduce your carbon footprint and transportation costs.

Local and Organic Food: Buy locally sourced and organic foods to support sustainable agriculture practices and reduce the environmental impact of long-distance shipping.

DIY and Homemade Products: Make your cleaning products, and personal care items, and even grow your food if space allows.

3. Set Green Spending Limits

Determine how much you're willing to spend in each category while maintaining your green living goals. Create limits for your green spending and stick to them. For example, you might set a budget for organic groceries or allocate a specific amount for eco-friendly home improvements.

4. Invest in Long-Term Savings

Many green living choices can lead to long-term savings. For instance, energy-efficient appliances may have a higher upfront cost but result in lower energy bills over time. Think of these investments as savings opportunities that will pay off in the future.

5. Plan Your Meals

Meal planning can be a game-changer for both green living and budgeting. By planning your meals, you can reduce food waste, buy in bulk, and make the most of your ingredients. Plus, it simplifies your grocery shopping and saves time.

6. Regularly Review and Adjust

Your green living budget should be flexible and subject to regular review. As you implement changes and discover new strategies, adjust your budget accordingly. Be open to finding new ways to save money while staying true to your sustainability goals.

7. Embrace DIY and Second-Hand Shopping

Get creative and resourceful. DIY projects and second-hand shopping can save you money and reduce waste. Refurbishing furniture, upcycling clothing, and repurposing items not only cut costs but also reduced the demand for new products.

8. Track Your Progress

Keep track of your spending and progress toward your green living goals. There are many budgeting apps and tools available to help you stay on top of your financial and environmental objectives.

In conclusion, creating a green living budget is all about finding a balance between your financial well-being and your commitment to sustainable living. With careful planning, prioritization, and creativity, you can live a greener life while saving money in the process. It's a win-win for your wallet and the planet.

Eco-Friendly Lifestyle Hacks

Making eco-friendly choices in your everyday life doesn't have to be a major overhaul. Small changes can add up to make a significant difference. Here are some eco-friendly lifestyle hacks that are not only simple but can also help you reduce your environmental footprint:

1. Reusable Shopping Bags

Swap single-use plastic bags for reusable shopping bags made of cloth or durable materials. Keep a few in your car or by the front door so you never forget them when you head to the store.

2. Reduce Water Waste

Conserve water by fixing leaky faucets, taking shorter showers, and turning off the tap while brushing your teeth. You can also collect rainwater for your garden and invest in low-flow showerheads and faucets.

3. Energy-Efficient Lighting

Switch to LED or CFL bulbs. They use significantly less energy and last longer than traditional incandescent bulbs. You'll save on your electricity bills while reducing your carbon footprint.

4. Unplug and Power Down

Electronics and appliances continue to draw power when they're plugged in, even if they're turned off. Unplug chargers and devices not in use, and consider using smart power strips to make it easier.

5. Green Transportation

Opt for walking, biking, carpooling, or using public transportation when possible. If you need a new car, consider a fuel-efficient or electric vehicle.

6. Meatless Mondays

Reduce your meat consumption by having a meatless day each week. Meat production has a significant environmental impact, so choosing plant-based meals can help lower your carbon footprint.

7. Composting

Start a compost bin for your kitchen scraps and yard waste. Composting not only reduces the amount of organic waste in landfills but also produces nutrient-rich soil for your garden.

8. Buy in Bulk

Reduce packaging waste by buying products in bulk. Bring your containers to stores that offer package-free options or purchase larger quantities of non-perishable items to minimize packaging.

9. Support Local and Sustainable Brands

When shopping, choose products from local and sustainable brands that prioritize ethical and eco-friendly practices. Look for certifications like Fair Trade, USDA Organic, or Rainforest Alliance.

10. Sustainable Cleaning

Make your cleaning products using simple, eco-friendly ingredients like vinegar, baking soda, and lemon juice. These alternatives are cost-effective, safe, and reduce the use of harsh chemicals in your home.

11. Reduce Paper Waste

Go digital whenever possible. Pay bills online, opt for e-statements, and use email instead of paper mail. When printing is necessary, use both sides of the paper.

12. Be Mindful of Food Waste

Plan your meals, use leftovers creatively, and be mindful of food expiration dates. By reducing food waste, you'll save money and resources.

13. Grow Your Food

If you have space, start a garden to grow your fruits and vegetables. It's not only a satisfying hobby but also a great way to enjoy fresh, locally sourced produce.

14. Second-Hand Shopping

Consider buying second-hand clothing, furniture, and other items. Thrift stores, consignment shops, and online marketplaces are treasure troves of gently used goods.

15. *Zero-Waste Bathroom*

Swap disposable razors for a safety razor, use a menstrual cup or reusable pads, and choose soap and shampoo bars instead of bottled products. These small changes reduce bathroom waste.

By incorporating these eco-friendly lifestyle hacks into your daily routine, you'll contribute to a more sustainable world while simplifying your life and, in many cases, saving money. It's proof that making a positive impact on the environment can be easy and accessible to everyone.

Small changes can add up to make a significant difference.

Chapter 3

The Importance of Sustainable Eating

Food and Environmental Impact

In this chapter, we delve into the heart of green living: sustainable eating. We'll explore the profound impact of our food choices on the environment and the reasons why it's vital to make more sustainable choices.

Food and Environmental Impact

Ever thought about the journey your food takes from farm to plate? It's a complex one, and it has a significant impact on our planet. Here's why it matters:

1. Carbon Footprint

The food industry is a major contributor to greenhouse gas emissions. From transportation and production to packaging and waste, the food we consume has a carbon footprint. Reducing meat and dairy consumption and choosing locally sourced, seasonal produce can significantly lower your food-related carbon emissions.

2. Land Use and Deforestation

Large-scale agriculture often involves clearing vast swaths of land for crop cultivation and animal farming. This leads to deforestation, which not only reduces biodiversity but also releases carbon stored in trees. Sustainable eating promotes practices that use land more efficiently and reduce the need for deforestation.

3. Water Consumption

Water is a precious resource, and traditional farming methods can be incredibly water-intensive. Sustainable eating encourages the responsible use of water resources in agriculture, conserving this vital element for future generations.

4. Biodiversity Loss

Monoculture farming, where a single crop is grown over vast areas, can lead to biodiversity loss. Sustainable practices, like supporting local and organic farming, help maintain diverse ecosystems and protect vital pollinators like bees.

5. Chemical Pollution

Conventional agriculture relies on pesticides and synthetic fertilizers, which can contaminate soil, and water, and harm non-target species. Sustainable eating favors organic farming methods, reducing the use of harmful chemicals and promoting healthier ecosystems.

6. Food Waste

One-third of all food produced globally is wasted. When we waste food, we also waste the resources used to grow, transport, and package it. Sustainable eating involves reducing food waste through better planning, storage, and creative use of leftovers.

7. Ocean Health

Seafood is a critical part of many diets, but overfishing and destructive fishing practices threaten the health of our oceans. Sustainable seafood choices and responsible fishing practices help protect marine ecosystems.

8. Human Health

Sustainable eating isn't just about the environment; it's about personal health too. By choosing nutritious, whole foods and reducing the consumption of processed and highly packaged products, you can improve your well-being.

9. Food Security

A sustainable food system is more resilient and better equipped to withstand environmental challenges like climate change. By supporting sustainable practices, you contribute to global food security.

10. Ethical Considerations

Sustainable eating is also about ethics. It's about choosing foods that align with your values, such as supporting fair labor practices, animal welfare, and equitable access to food resources.

In conclusion, what you put on your plate has far-reaching implications for the environment, our health, and the global food system. Sustainable eating is a commitment to making choices that not only nourish your body but also protect the planet and promote a more just and equitable food system. It's about recognizing the power you hold with every bite and making choices that reflect your values and contribute to a better world.

The Ethics of Food Choices

Food isn't just fuel for our bodies; it's a reflection of our values, culture, and the impact we have on the world. The ethics of food choices go beyond personal preferences, extending to considerations of the environment, animal welfare, and social justice. Here, we delve into the ethical dimensions of what we eat and why it matters.

1. Environmental Impact

One of the most significant ethical considerations in food choices is the impact on the environment. Traditional agriculture practices, with their heavy use of synthetic pesticides and fertilizers, can degrade soil, harm water systems, and contribute to climate change. Ethical food choices favor practices that minimize these environmental harms, such as supporting organic farming, reducing meat consumption, and choosing locally sourced produce.

2. Animal Welfare

The treatment of animals in the food industry raises profound ethical questions. Factory farming, where animals are often subjected to inhumane conditions and practices, challenges our moral compass. Ethical food choices include opting for humanely raised and slaughtered meat, supporting cage-free egg production, and choosing products from companies that prioritize animal welfare.

3. Fair Trade

Global food systems are complex and often involve the exploitation of labor in developing countries. Ethical food choices include supporting fair trade products, which ensure that farmers and workers receive fair compensation and have decent working conditions. This promotes economic justice and helps lift communities out of poverty.

4. Local and Sustainable Practices

Choosing local and sustainable food options can have a positive impact on your community. It supports local farmers and reduces the carbon footprint associated with transporting food over long distances. It also encourages sustainable land use and fosters biodiversity in your region.

5. Food Justice

Food deserts, areas where fresh, healthy food is inaccessible, are a stark reality in many communities. Ethical food choices involve advocating for food justice by supporting efforts to increase access to nutritious, affordable food for all, regardless of their socioeconomic status.

6. Cultural Respect

Food is an integral part of culture and identity. Respecting and preserving traditional food practices and culinary heritage is an ethical choice. It acknowledges the value of cultural diversity and the importance of food in shaping our sense of self.

7. Reducing Waste

Food waste is a global concern with ethical implications. By reducing food waste, you not only save money but also contribute to the responsible use of resources and reduce the environmental impact of waste disposal.

8. Sustainable Seafood Choices

Overfishing and destructive fishing practices have depleted marine life. Ethical food choices extend to seafood by supporting sustainable fishing practices and choosing seafood options that are not threatened or overfished.

9. Personal Health

Taking care of your health is an ethical consideration too. By choosing foods that nourish your body and reduce the risk of diet-related diseases, you minimize the burden on healthcare systems and contribute to a healthier society.

In summary, ethical food choices are a powerful way to express your values and promote a better world. They encompass considerations of the environment, animal welfare, social justice, and personal health. By making conscious choices that reflect your ethics, you can be part of a global movement toward a more just and sustainable food system that benefits us all.

Sustainable Eating Benefits

Choosing sustainable eating habits isn't just about being environmentally conscious; it also offers a multitude of personal, societal, and global advantages. Here are the compelling benefits of adopting a sustainable approach to your diet:

1. Environmental Preservation

Sustainable eating significantly reduces your environmental impact. By consuming locally sourced and organic foods, you help decrease greenhouse gas emissions, minimize water usage, and promote land conservation, contributing to a healthier planet.

2. Healthier Lifestyle

Opting for whole, plant-based foods can positively impact your health. A diet rich in fruits, vegetables, whole grains, and legumes is linked to reduced risk of chronic diseases like heart disease, diabetes, and certain cancers.

3. Support for Local Economies

Choosing locally grown produce and supporting small-scale farmers helps boost local economies. It encourages community engagement, sustains local agricultural traditions, and provides economic support to nearby farmers.

4. Animal Welfare

By selecting sustainably sourced animal products, such as grass-fed beef or cage-free eggs, you support practices that are more humane to animals. This ethical consideration aligns with the principles of compassionate living.

5. Reduced Food Waste

Sustainable eating often involves a more mindful approach to food consumption. Being aware of where your food comes from, how it's produced, and reducing food waste helps minimize the overall wastage in the food supply chain.

6. Economic Savings

Believe it or not, sustainable eating can save you money. Choosing seasonal, local produce and reducing meat consumption can lead to cost savings. Additionally, growing your food, buying in bulk, and reducing food waste contribute to economic benefits.

7. Diverse and Nutritious Diet

Focusing on a diverse range of foods, especially plant-based options, introduces a variety of nutrients into your diet. Sustainable eating encourages a more colorful plate, offering a broader spectrum of vitamins, minerals, and antioxidants.

8. Food Security

Promoting sustainable agricultural practices helps ensure a stable and secure food supply. By diversifying crops and supporting sustainable farming methods, we strengthen our ability to meet global food demands, reducing the risk of food shortages.

9. Community and Social Connection

Engaging in sustainable eating often involves participating in community-supported agriculture, farmers' markets, and sharing resources with neighbors. This not only supports local businesses but also fosters social connections within the community.

10. Personal Fulfillment

Knowing that your food choices are making a positive impact on the environment and society can bring a sense of fulfillment and purpose. It's empowering to know that your actions contribute to a more sustainable world.

In essence, the benefits of sustainable eating extend far beyond personal health. They encompass global, environmental, and societal advantages, all of which align with a more ethical and mindful way of living. By embracing sustainable eating practices, you not only nourish yourself but also contribute to a healthier planet and community for generations to come.

Chapter 4

Budget-Friendly Green Eating

Smart Grocery Shopping

Welcome to the heart of practical sustainability – budget-friendly green eating. Here, we'll explore strategies to make eco-conscious food choices without breaking the bank. It all starts with smart grocery shopping.

Smart Grocery Shopping

Your journey towards budget-friendly green eating begins in the grocery store. This chapter unveils tips and tricks for making conscious, sustainable, and economical food choices.

1. Make a List and Stick to It

One of the simplest yet most effective grocery shopping strategies is to make a list before you head to the store. Planning your meals for the week and listing the ingredients you need not only saves time but also ensures you buy only what you require. It helps reduce food waste and keeps your budget in check.

2. Buy in Season

Seasonal produce is not only fresher and tastier but also more affordable. When fruits and vegetables are in season, they're abundant, making them a cost-effective choice. Plus, supporting local, seasonal produce is a cornerstone of sustainable eating.

3. Embrace Plant-Based Proteins

Plant-based proteins like beans, lentils, and tofu are not only budget-friendly but also more eco-friendly than many animal-based protein sources. They're versatile, nutritious, and a sustainable choice for your health and the environment.

4. Shop in Bulk

Buying in bulk, when possible, can save you money and reduce packaging waste. Look for stores or co-ops that offer bulk bins for grains, nuts, seeds, and dried fruits.

Bring your containers to fill and weigh them at checkout.

5. Choose Store Brands

Store-brand products are often more affordable than name brands and are of comparable quality. Opt for store brands whenever possible to save money without sacrificing quality.

6. Minimize Processed Foods

Processed and convenience foods tend to be pricier and less environmentally friendly due to excessive packaging. Choosing whole, unprocessed foods not only reduces costs but also supports a healthier and more sustainable diet.

7. Limit Impulse Buys

Impulse purchases can quickly derail your budget. Stick to your shopping list and avoid aisles that tempt you with items you don't need. This discipline not only saves money but also reduces the resources associated with producing unnecessary items.

8. Comparison Shop

Don't hesitate to compare prices among different brands and sizes of products. What's on sale? Which package size offers the best value? Spending a few extra moments comparing can lead to significant savings.

9. Stock Up on Staples

Items like rice, pasta, canned tomatoes, and frozen vegetables are essential staples that can be purchased in larger quantities when on sale. They have long shelf lives and can serve as the foundation for various meals.

10. Use Coupons and Discounts

Take advantage of coupons, discounts, and loyalty programs offered by your grocery store. Apps and websites often provide digital coupons that can be clipped for extra savings.

11. Avoid Single-Use Plastics

Look for products with minimal or no plastic packaging to reduce your plastic waste. When you do use plastic, make sure it's recyclable or can be repurposed.

12. Read Labels

Before you buy, check labels for information on organic, non-GMO, and Fair Trade certifications. These labels can guide your choices toward more sustainable and ethical products.

By adopting these smart grocery shopping practices, you can make budget-friendly green eating a reality in your daily life. It's a win-win situation: you save money, reduce waste, and make eco-conscious food choices that support a healthier planet.

Meal Planning for Sustainability

Meal planning is not just about organizing your week's meals; it's a powerful tool for sustainable eating. Here's how you can make meal planning an integral part of your eco-friendly lifestyle:

1. Reduce Food Waste

Planning your meals in advance allows you to buy only what you need. By creating a detailed grocery list based on your meal plan, you can avoid unnecessary purchases and reduce food waste. Utilize leftovers effectively by incorporating them into future meals, minimizing the amount of discarded food.

2. Choose Plant-Based Options

Incorporate more plant-based meals into your plan. Plant-based diets have a lower environmental impact, reducing greenhouse gas emissions, water usage, and land degradation. Opting for plant-based protein sources like legumes, tofu, or tempeh can significantly decrease your carbon footprint.

3. Support Local and Seasonal Produce

Base your meal plan on seasonal and locally sourced produce. Not only are these foods fresher and more nutritious, but they also support local farmers and reduce the carbon emissions associated with long-distance transportation.

4. Diversify Your Meals

Variety in your meal plan not only adds excitement to your diet but also helps spread the environmental impact. Avoid over-reliance on a few key ingredients, as this can strain specific resources. Experiment with a wide array of grains, fruits, vegetables, and legumes.

5. Opt for Bulk Ingredients

When planning your meals, consider using bulk ingredients. Items like grains, nuts, seeds, and dried fruits purchased in bulk reduce packaging waste and are often more cost-effective.

6. Cook in Batches

Preparing larger quantities of food and storing leftovers for future meals not only saves time but also reduces energy usage. Cooking in batches is more efficient and minimizes the need for continuous heating and cooling.

7. Embrace DIY and Homemade

Make your own sauces, dressings, and snacks. This not only saves money but also reduces the number of single-use plastic containers or packaging from store-bought items.

8. Utilize Sustainable Cooking Methods

Choose cooking methods that are more energy-efficient. Opt for using the microwave, pressure cooker, or slow cooker, which tends to use less energy than traditional ovens or stovetops.

9. Plan for a Zero-Waste Kitchen

Consider meal planning as an opportunity to aim for a zero-waste kitchen. Use the entire vegetable, including stems and peels, in creative and delicious ways. Compost food scraps and ensure you're making the most of the resources you purchase.

10. Flexibility and Adaptability

Be flexible in your meal planning. Things don't always go as planned and produce may ripen sooner than expected. Be adaptable and ready to adjust your meal plan to prevent food from going to waste.

11. Learn Preservation Techniques

Explore food preservation techniques like freezing, canning, or pickling. These methods extend the life of produce and prevent spoilage, allowing you to use seasonal foods throughout the year.

Meal planning for sustainability is about more than just organizing your weekly menu; it's a conscious and intentional approach to reducing waste, making eco-friendly food choices, and supporting a more sustainable food system. By incorporating these strategies into your meal planning, you can contribute to a healthier planet while enjoying delicious, nourishing meals.

Reducing Food Waste

Food waste is a significant global problem, and it has far-reaching economic, environmental, and ethical implications. Reducing food waste is not only an eco-friendly practice but also a way to save money and ensure food resources are distributed more equitably. Here are some strategies to help you minimize food waste in your daily life:

1. Plan Your Meals

Meal planning is one of the most effective ways to reduce food waste. By planning your meals, you can create a shopping list with only the items you need, reducing the chances of buying excessive food that may go to waste.

2. Use Leftovers Creatively

Leftovers don't have to be boring. Get creative and repurpose them into new meals. For example, last night's roasted vegetables can become a delicious frittata, and cooked rice can be transformed into a stir-fry.

3. Practice FIFO (First In, First Out)

When storing food, follow the FIFO method. Consume older items before newer ones. This ensures that food with a shorter shelf life is used first.

4. Proper Storage

Proper storage is crucial for extending the life of your food. Use airtight containers for leftovers, and store fruits and vegetables in the right conditions – some require refrigeration, while others should be stored at room temperature.

5. Composting

Create a compost bin for food scraps that can't be used. Composting not only reduces food waste but also produces nutrient-rich soil for your garden.

6. Be Mindful of Expiration Dates

Expiry dates on food packaging are often conservative estimates. Use your senses, like sight, smell, and taste, to determine if a food item is still safe to eat. Trust your judgment before discarding something based solely on its expiration date.

7. Avoid Overbuying

Buying in bulk can be cost-effective, but it can also lead to food waste if you purchase more than you can consume. Buy in larger quantities only if you have the means to store and use the items efficiently.

8. Freeze Perishables

If you have fruits, vegetables, or other perishables that you can't consume in time, freeze them. This preserves their freshness and extends their usability.

9. Donate Excess Food

Consider donating excess non-perishable and unspoiled food items to local food banks or organizations that help those in need.

10. Portion Control

Be mindful of portion sizes when cooking or serving meals. Avoid over-serving, which can lead to uneaten food on plates.

11. Educate Yourself

Learn about the differences between "best before" and "use by" dates, and understand food storage and preservation techniques. Education is key to reducing food waste.

12. Support Businesses Reducing Food Waste

Support restaurants, cafes, and grocery stores that have implemented food waste reduction initiatives. Encourage businesses to donate surplus food to charities rather than discard it.

13. Repurpose Scraps

Don't throw away food scraps like vegetable peels, bones, or stale bread. Use them to make broths, stocks, and croutons, reducing waste and adding flavor to your dishes.

By adopting these practices, you can significantly reduce your food waste, which not only benefits your wallet but also the environment. It's a small but impactful step toward a more sustainable and responsible approach to food consumption.

Reducing food waste is not only an eco-friendly practice but also a way to save money and ensure food resources are distributed more equitably.

Chapter 5

Green Kitchen Practices

Energy-Efficient Cooking

Food waste is a significant global problem, and it has far-reaching economic, environmental, and ethical implications. Reducing food waste is not only an eco-friendly practice but also a way to save money and ensure food resources are distributed more equitably. Here are some strategies to help you minimize food waste in your daily life:

1. Plan Your Meals

Meal planning is one of the most effective ways to reduce food waste. By planning your meals, you can create a shopping list with only the items you need, reducing the chances of buying excessive food that may go to waste.

2. Use Leftovers Creatively

Leftovers don't have to be boring. Get creative and repurpose them into new meals. For example, last night's roasted vegetables can become a delicious frittata, and cooked rice can be transformed into a stir-fry.

3. Practice FIFO (First In, First Out)

When storing food, follow the FIFO method. Consume older items before newer ones. This ensures that food with a shorter shelf life is used first.

4. Proper Storage

Proper storage is crucial for extending the life of your food. Use airtight containers for leftovers, and store fruits and vegetables in the right conditions - some require refrigeration, while others should be stored at room temperature.

5. Composting

Create a compost bin for food scraps that can't be used. Composting not only reduces food waste but also produces nutrient-rich soil for your garden.

6. Be Mindful of Expiration Dates

Expiry dates on food packaging are often conservative estimates. Use your senses, like sight, smell, and taste, to determine if a food item is still safe to eat. Trust your judgment before discarding something based solely on its expiration date.

7. Avoid Overbuying

Buying in bulk can be cost-effective, but it can also lead to food waste if you purchase more than you can consume. Buy in larger quantities only if you have the means to store and use the items efficiently.

8. Freeze Perishables

If you have fruits, vegetables, or other perishables that you can't consume in time, freeze them. This preserves their freshness and extends their usability.

9. Donate Excess Food

Consider donating excess non-perishable and unspoiled food items to local food banks or organizations that help those in need.

10. Portion Control

Be mindful of portion sizes when cooking or serving meals. Avoid over-serving, which can lead to uneaten food on plates.

11. Educate Yourself

Learn about the differences between "best before" and "use by" dates, and understand food storage and preservation techniques. Education is key to reducing food waste.

12. Support Businesses Reducing Food Waste

Support restaurants, cafes, and grocery stores that have implemented food waste reduction initiatives. Encourage businesses to donate surplus food to charities rather than discard it.

And

Don't throw away food scraps like vegetable peels, bones, or stale bread. Use them to make broths, stocks, and croutons, reducing waste and adding flavor to your dishes.

By adopting these practices, you can significantly reduce your food waste, which not only benefits your wallet but also the environment. It's a small but impactful step toward a more sustainable and responsible approach to food consumption.

Reducing Plastic in the Kitchen

Plastic pollution is a global environmental concern, and the kitchen is a hotspot for plastic use. Reducing plastic in the kitchen not only helps the planet but also promotes a healthier and more sustainable lifestyle. Here are practical steps to minimize plastic usage in your culinary space:

1. Use Reusable Shopping Bags

Ditch single-use plastic bags in favor of reusable, eco-friendly bags. Keep a few of them in your car or near the front door for grocery shopping trips.

2. Choose Glass or Stainless Steel Containers

Opt for glass or stainless steel containers for storing food. These materials are durable, long-lasting, and won't leach harmful chemicals into your food.

3. Reusable Water Bottles

Invest in a reusable water bottle made from stainless steel, glass, or other non-plastic materials. This reduces the need for disposable plastic water bottles.

4. Eco-Friendly Food Wraps

Replace plastic cling wrap with eco-friendly alternatives like beeswax wraps or silicone lids. These can effectively cover and preserve your food without waste.

5. Say No to Disposable Cutlery and Plates

Avoid disposable plastic cutlery, plates, and cups. Instead, use reusable silverware, dishes, and glasses, even when dining outdoors or during picnics.

6. Choose Natural Fiber Dishcloths

Opt for natural fiber dishcloths made of cotton or bamboo instead of synthetic sponges and scrubbers. When they wear out, they can be composted.

7. Use Bar Soap

Replace liquid hand soap in plastic bottles with bar soap. Bar soap often comes with minimal or no packaging and lasts longer.

8. Buy in Bulk

Purchase pantry staples like rice, pasta, and spices in bulk. Many stores offer these items in dispensers, allowing you to bring your containers and reduce packaging waste.

9. Make Homemade Cleaning Products

Create your cleaning solutions using simple, eco-friendly ingredients like vinegar, baking soda, and essential oils. This reduces the need for plastic bottles of cleaning products.

10. Avoid Plastic Packaging

When shopping for groceries, look for items with minimal plastic packaging. Choose loose produce or items in paper, glass, or cardboard packaging.

11. Compost Food Scraps

If you're discarding fruit and vegetable scraps or coffee grounds, consider composting them instead of using plastic garbage bags. Composting diverts organic waste from landfills and enriches your garden soil.

12. Opt for Non-Plastic Kitchen Tools

Select non-plastic kitchen utensils and tools, like wooden or metal spatulas and stirring spoons. They are more durable and sustainable.

13. Buy in Glass or Metal

When possible, choose beverages and condiments in glass or metal containers rather than plastic. These are more readily recyclable and have fewer environmental impacts.

14. Reduce Plastic Food Storage

Instead of using plastic bags and containers for food storage, repurpose glass jars or invest in silicone food storage bags and glass containers with plastic-free lids.

15. Support Plastic-Free Brands

Support companies that prioritize plastic reduction and offer plastic-free packaging. By voting with your wallet, you can encourage more businesses to adopt eco-friendly practices.

Reducing plastic in the kitchen is not just about eliminating waste; it's a way to live more sustainably and contribute to a healthier planet. By making conscious choices in your culinary space, you can significantly decrease your plastic footprint and inspire others to do the same.

Growing Your Own Food

There's something deeply rewarding and satisfying about tending to your garden and harvesting the fruits (and vegetables) of your labor. Growing your food not only connects you with nature but also offers a multitude of benefits for your health, wallet, and the environment. Here's why you should consider embracing this green thumb lifestyle:

1. Fresh and Nutritious Produce

Homegrown fruits and vegetables are at their peak of freshness when harvested. This means they're packed with nutrients and often taste better than their store-bought counterparts. You have the freedom to choose what you grow, ensuring that your family enjoys a diverse and nutritious diet.

2. Reduced Environmental Impact

Growing your food can significantly reduce your carbon footprint. You don't have to rely on the transportation and packaging associated with store-bought produce. Plus, you have control over the use of pesticides and fertilizers, allowing you to employ eco-friendly gardening practices.

3. Cost Savings

While there's an initial investment in gardening supplies and tools, growing your food can save you money in the long run. The cost of seeds and soil amendments is often minimal compared to the price of store-bought organic produce.

4. Connection to Nature

Gardening provides a connection to the natural world that's often missing in our modern lives. It's a therapeutic and grounding activity that allows you to disconnect from screens and reconnect with the earth.

5. Food Security

Your garden can act as a source of food security. In times of economic uncertainty or emergencies, having access to homegrown produce can be invaluable.

6. Educational Opportunity

If you have children, involving them in gardening is a fantastic educational experience. They'll learn about plant life cycles, ecosystems, and the joy of growing their food. It's a lesson in sustainability that can last a lifetime.

7. Reduce Food Miles

When you grow your food, you're essentially eliminating "food miles." This term refers to the distance food travels from farm to plate. By eating local and homegrown produce, you reduce the environmental impact associated with long-distance transportation.

8. Control Over Pesticides and Chemicals

You have control over what goes into your garden, including the use of pesticides and chemicals. If you choose to follow organic or chemical-free gardening methods, you can ensure that your food is free from harmful residues.

9. Self-Sufficiency

Growing your food can make you more self-sufficient. You'll rely less on external sources for your meals and can take pride in providing for your family from your garden.

10. Food Diversity

You can grow a wide variety of fruits, vegetables, herbs, and even edible flowers in your garden. This diversity not only adds culinary excitement to your meals but also contributes to biodiversity and supports pollinators.

11. Stress Reduction

Gardening is known for its stress-reducing qualities. It offers a chance to unwind, immerse yourself in a different world, and connect with nature – all of which can have a positive impact on your overall well-being.

Whether you have a sprawling backyard or a small balcony, there are gardening options for everyone. Container gardening, vertical gardening, or traditional garden beds are all ways to get started.

Chapter 6

Holistic Health and Green Living

Connecting Your Health to the Environment

In this chapter, we explore the deep connections between our health and the environment, highlighting the intricate relationship between personal well-being and sustainable living.

Connecting Your Health to the Environment

Our health is intricately intertwined with the health of the environment. Recognizing this connection is fundamental to embracing a holistic approach to well-being and green living. Here's how the two are deeply linked:

1. Nutrient-Rich, Sustainable Diets

A diet rich in whole, sustainably sourced foods not only nurtures your body but also reduces the environmental impact of your eating habits. Choosing locally grown, organic, and plant-based foods not only benefits your health but also supports sustainable agricultural practices.

2. Reduction of Toxins and Chemicals

Limiting exposure to harmful chemicals and toxins in the environment has a direct impact on personal health. By opting for organic produce and eco-friendly household products, you reduce the intake of harmful substances and contribute to a cleaner environment.

3. Outdoor Activities and Well-Being

Engaging in outdoor activities not only promotes physical fitness but also connects you to nature. It fosters a sense of well-being, reduces stress, and encourages an appreciation for the natural world.

4. Clean Air and Mental Health

Air quality significantly impacts mental and physical health. By advocating for cleaner air through reduced pollution and support for green spaces, you're contributing to better mental well-being for yourself and your community.

5. Access to Green Spaces

Access to parks, gardens, and natural landscapes is linked to better health outcomes. By supporting and advocating for green spaces, you contribute to community health and well-being.

6. Sustainable Exercise Practices

Choosing sustainable modes of exercise, like walking or cycling, reduces your carbon footprint while benefiting your health. These activities promote fitness without contributing to environmental degradation.

7. Mindful Consumerism

Understanding the impact of your consumer choices on both personal health and the environment is crucial. By being mindful of the products you use, from food to household items, you contribute to a healthier environment and lifestyle.

8. Stress Reduction through Green Living

Green living practices, such as gardening, nature walks, or even mindful recycling, have stress-reducing qualities. Stress has significant impacts on health, and connecting with nature can alleviate these effects.

9. Climate Change and Health

Recognizing the health risks associated with climate change is part of understanding the environmental impact on personal well-being. Extreme weather events, air pollution, and changing disease patterns all affect human health.

10. Community Engagement and Support

Engaging with and supporting community initiatives that promote health and sustainability fosters a sense of belonging and collective well-being. These shared efforts benefit both individuals and the environment.

Understanding the connections between personal health and the environment is fundamental to embracing a holistic approach to well-being. By adopting green living practices, supporting sustainable initiatives, and advocating for a healthier environment, you not only improve your health but also contribute to a more sustainable and resilient world for future generations.

Eco-Friendly Personal Care

Caring for yourself doesn't have to come at the expense of the planet. Eco-friendly personal care is a thoughtful approach to personal well-being that minimizes environmental impact. Here are some ways to make your personal care routine more sustainable:

1. Use Natural and Biodegradable Products

Opt for personal care products made from natural and biodegradable ingredients. Look for shampoos, soaps, and skincare items that are free from harsh chemicals and synthetic fragrances, as these can harm both your health and the environment.

2. Minimal Packaging

Choose products with minimal packaging or packaging made from recyclable or biodegradable materials. Avoid single-use plastics and opt for refillable containers when possible.

3. Reusable Toiletries

Replace disposable items with reusable alternatives. For instance, use washable cloth wipes instead of disposable makeup remover pads, and opt for a safety razor instead of disposable plastic razors.

4. Support Eco-Friendly Brands

Seek out brands that prioritize sustainability in their products and packaging. Many companies are now adopting eco-friendly practices and offering green alternatives.

5. DIY Personal Care

Consider making your personal care products like toothpaste, deodorant, or face masks. This way, you have control over the ingredients and can minimize waste.

6. Choose Sustainable Packaging

When selecting personal care products, consider the type of packaging. Glass, metal, or cardboard packaging is often more eco-friendly than plastic. Look for products that offer recyclable or refillable options.

7. Energy-Efficient Grooming

Conserve energy by using energy-efficient grooming tools, like low-flow showerheads, and by taking shorter showers. These small changes add up to significant water and energy savings over time.

8. Mindful Water Usage

Be mindful of water consumption during personal care routines. Turn off the tap while brushing your teeth or lathering your hands and use a water-saving showerhead.

9. Natural Fiber and Organic Textiles

Choose natural fiber and organic textiles for personal care items like towels and washcloths. Organic cotton or bamboo textiles are not only gentle on your skin but also more sustainable choices.

10. Eco-Friendly Cosmetics

Look for cosmetics with natural and organic ingredients. Many brands now offer sustainable makeup options that are cruelty-free and free from harmful chemicals.

11. Eco-Friendly Cleaning

Choose eco-friendly cleaning products for personal care items. Avoid products with harsh chemicals that can harm the environment and water systems.

12. Donate Unused Products

If you have personal care products that you no longer need or use, consider donating them to shelters or organizations that can put them to good use.

13. Compostable and Biodegradable Items

Use compostable or biodegradable personal care items, such as cotton swabs with paper stems and biodegradable dental floss.

By adopting eco-friendly personal care practices, you can take care of yourself while minimizing your environmental impact. Making sustainable choices in your daily routine not only benefits the planet but also contributes to your overall well-being and health.

Exercise and Sustainable Living

Engaging in physical activity not only promotes personal health but also aligns with sustainable living practices. Here's how exercise and sustainability intersect, offering benefits for both individuals and the environment:

1. Active Commuting

Choosing active modes of transportation like walking, cycling, or using public transport not only reduces carbon emissions but also contributes to your daily exercise. It's a win-win for personal health and the environment.

2. Outdoor Exercise

Opt for outdoor activities like hiking, jogging, or outdoor sports. Exercising in natural settings not only benefits your physical fitness but also fosters a deeper connection to nature, nurturing an appreciation for the environment.

3. Fitness and Well-Being

Regular physical activity promotes overall well-being. By maintaining a healthy and active lifestyle, you're more likely to make conscious choices that support sustainable living practices.

4. Energy-Efficient Gyms

Gyms that prioritize energy-efficient practices and use sustainable materials contribute to a greener environment. Choosing eco-friendly gyms supports sustainability in the fitness industry.

5. Mindful Consumption

Engaging in exercise encourages mindfulness about consumption. Whether it's opting for durable workout gear or supporting eco-friendly fitness brands, the mindset developed through exercise can extend to other sustainable choices in life.

6. Staying Healthy to Support Sustainability Efforts

Staying healthy and fit enables you to contribute more actively to sustainability efforts. Whether it's participating in community clean-ups, conservation projects, or advocating for environmental policies, good health allows for greater involvement.

7. Conserving Resources

Being physically active often leads to more conscientious use of resources. When you're attuned to the benefits of exercise, you're more likely to conserve resources like water, electricity, and fuel in your daily life.

8. Supporting Green Events

Participating in eco-friendly sports events, races, or outdoor fitness gatherings supports sustainability initiatives. Many such events prioritize eco-friendly practices like recycling, minimizing waste, and reducing their carbon footprint.

9. Promoting Mental Health

Regular exercise is known to support mental health. When people feel mentally well, they are more likely to make positive choices that benefit themselves and the environment.

Chapter 7

Green Home and Cleaning

Non-Toxic Cleaning Products

In this chapter, we delve into the world of creating an environmentally friendly home, with a particular focus on using non-toxic cleaning products that are safe for both your family and the planet.

Non-Toxic Cleaning Products

Cleaning is an essential part of home maintenance, but it doesn't have to come at the cost of environmental health or personal well-being. By choosing non-toxic cleaning products, you can create a cleaner, safer, and greener living space. Here's how to make the switch:

1. Understand the Risks of Conventional Cleaners

Conventional cleaning products often contain harsh chemicals that can be harmful when inhaled or come into contact with the skin. These chemicals can also harm the environment when they wash down the drain.

2. Read Labels

Before buying any cleaning product, read the labels. Look for products that are free from harmful chemicals like ammonia, bleach, phthalates, and synthetic fragrances. Instead, opt for items that list natural, biodegradable ingredients.

3. Make Your Own Cleaners

Consider making your non-toxic cleaners using simple ingredients like vinegar, baking soda, lemon juice, and essential oils. Homemade cleaners are effective, cost-efficient, and reduce waste associated with packaging.

4. Choose Green Cleaning Brands

Look for brands that prioritize eco-friendly and non-toxic formulations. Many companies now offer a range of green cleaning products that are readily available in stores or online.

5. Go Minimalist

You don't need a different cleaning product for every surface or task. A few versatile, non-toxic cleaning products can handle most household cleaning needs. This reduces waste and simplifies your cleaning routine.

6. Reduce Plastic Waste

Consider purchasing non-toxic cleaning products in bulk or larger quantities to reduce packaging waste. Many brands offer concentrated forms that can be diluted with water.

7. Safe Disposal

When disposing of old or unused cleaning products, follow local guidelines for hazardous waste disposal. Many communities have specific programs for safely disposing of household chemicals.

8. Prioritize Eco-Friendly Packaging

Choose cleaning products with minimal and eco-friendly packaging. Look for options with recyclable or biodegradable containers.

9. Research Cleaning Methods

Different cleaning methods may require varying products. Research effective and environmentally friendly cleaning methods for different surfaces, such as glass, countertops, or floors.

10. Educate Yourself

Stay informed about the potential dangers of toxic cleaning products and the benefits of non-toxic alternatives. Knowledge is your best ally in making informed choices.

11. Eco-Friendly Cleaning Tools

Use eco-friendly cleaning tools like microfiber cloths, reusable mop pads, and scrub brushes with biodegradable or recycled materials.

12. Ventilate While Cleaning

When using any cleaning product, ensure proper ventilation by opening windows or using exhaust fans. Adequate ventilation helps reduce indoor air pollution.

13. *Safety First*

Keep non-toxic cleaning products out of reach of children and pets. While they may be safer than traditional cleaners, they should still be handled with care.

By choosing non-toxic cleaning products, you not only create a safer and healthier home environment for your family but also contribute to a cleaner planet. These choices minimize exposure to harmful chemicals, reduce plastic waste, and support a more sustainable way of living. It's a step towards a greener, healthier, and more eco-conscious home.

Creating a Healthy Home Environment

Your home is more than just a place to sleep; it's where you and your family spend a significant portion of your lives. Creating a healthy home environment is essential for physical, mental, and emotional well-being. Here are some steps to ensure your home supports a healthy lifestyle:

1. Clean Indoor Air

Indoor air quality can significantly impact your health. To maintain clean air, use air purifiers, ensure proper ventilation, and avoid smoking indoors. Houseplants can also help filter the air.

2. Reduce Toxins

Minimize exposure to toxins by using non-toxic cleaning products and paints. Choose furniture and flooring made from natural materials to limit the off-gassing of harmful chemicals.

3. Control Moisture

A damp home can lead to mold growth, which can affect your respiratory health. Use dehumidifiers to control moisture levels, and promptly address any leaks or water damage.

4. Natural Light

Maximize natural light in your home. Exposure to natural light can improve mood and regulate sleep patterns. It's also an energy-efficient way to brighten your living space.

5. Green Living Plants

Incorporate green living plants into your decor. They not only purify the air but also bring a touch of nature indoors, improving overall well-being.

6. Reduce Clutter

Clutter can contribute to stress and anxiety. Create an organized living space that promotes a sense of calm and well-being.

7. Eco-Friendly Cleaning

Use eco-friendly cleaning products and methods. Harsh chemicals can linger in the air and on surfaces, potentially affecting your health.

8. Minimize Noise Pollution

Consider ways to reduce noise pollution in your home. Soundproofing, soft furnishings, and acoustic panels can create a quieter and more relaxing atmosphere.

9. Healthy Eating Space

Create a dedicated space for healthy eating. A clean, well-organized kitchen encourages nutritious meal preparation and family meals.

10. Natural Materials

Opt for furniture and decor made from natural materials like wood, bamboo, or cork. These materials are more sustainable and free from harmful chemicals.

11. Avoid Synthetic Fragrances

Synthetic fragrances in candles, air fresheners, and cleaning products can contribute to indoor air pollution. Choose unscented or naturally scented alternatives.

12. Water Quality

Ensure that your tap water is safe to drink. Consider a water filtration system to remove impurities and chemicals.

13. Maintain a Pest-Free Home

Pest control can introduce harmful chemicals into your home. Use eco-friendly pest control methods and keep your home well-sealed to prevent pests from entering.

14. Create Relaxation Spaces

Designate areas in your home for relaxation and stress relief. Whether it's a cozy reading nook, a meditation space, or a comfortable bath, having areas for relaxation can support your mental and emotional health.

15. Family Engagement

Involve your family in creating a healthy home. Teach children the importance of sustainable living, healthy eating, and eco-conscious practices.

16. Reduce Energy Consumption

Reducing energy consumption not only saves you money but also lowers your environmental impact. Use energy-efficient appliances, seal drafts, and consider solar panels to power your home.

Creating a healthy home environment is an ongoing process that involves thoughtful choices and a commitment to well-being. A healthy home supports not only physical health but also mental and emotional health, contributing to a happier and more sustainable lifestyle.

Energy-Efficient Living

In a world increasingly concerned with environmental sustainability and the rising costs of energy, energy-efficient living is more than just a trend, it's a responsible and cost-effective way of life. Here's how you can embrace energy-efficient living to reduce your carbon footprint and save money:

1. Energy-Efficient Appliances

Invest in energy-efficient appliances. Look for the ENERGY STAR label, which signifies that a product meets specific energy efficiency criteria. Energy-efficient appliances consume less electricity, reducing both your energy bills and environmental impact.

2. LED Lighting

Replace traditional incandescent bulbs with LED lighting. LED bulbs last longer, use less energy, and produce less heat, making them a smart choice for reducing electricity consumption.

3. Smart Thermostats

Install a programmable or smart thermostat. These devices allow you to adjust your home's temperature based on your schedule, ensuring that you're not heating or cooling an empty house.

4. Proper Insulation

Ensure your home is well-insulated. Proper insulation reduces heat loss in the winter and keeps your home cooler in the summer, reducing the need for heating and air conditioning.

5. Energy-Efficient Windows

Consider energy-efficient windows that are designed to minimize heat transfer. They can significantly improve your home's insulation and help maintain a consistent indoor temperature.

6. Seal Air Leaks

Inspect your home for air leaks around windows, doors, and vents. Seal these gaps to prevent drafts, which can make your heating and cooling systems work harder.

7. Solar Power

If feasible, invest in solar panels to generate your clean energy. Solar power can not only reduce your electricity bills but also allow you to sell excess energy back to the grid.

8. Unplug Electronics

Unplug chargers, appliances, and electronics when they're not in use. Many devices continue to draw power, even when turned off, in a phenomenon known as "vampire" or "phantom" power consumption.

9. Energy-Efficient Water Heating

Install an energy-efficient water heater. Tankless water heaters, for example, heat water on demand, reducing standby energy loss.

10. Energy-Efficient Landscaping

Plant trees and shrubs strategically to provide shade to your home in the summer, reducing the need for air conditioning. In the winter, they can act as windbreaks, reducing heat loss.

11. Regular Maintenance

Maintain your heating, cooling, and ventilation systems regularly. A well-maintained system operates more efficiently and lasts longer.

12. Reduce, Reuse, Recycle

Consume less by adopting a "reduce, reuse, recycle" mindset. The less you consume, the fewer resources you use, and the less energy is needed to produce and transport goods.

13. Efficient Transportation

Choose energy-efficient transportation options, like carpooling, biking, walking, or using public transport. If possible, consider switching to an electric or hybrid vehicle.

14. Energy-Efficient Cooking

Use energy-efficient cooking methods like pressure cookers, slow cookers, and microwave ovens, which consume less energy than conventional stovetops and ovens.

15. Education and Advocacy

Stay informed about energy-efficient practices and technologies. Advocate for energy efficiency in your community and support policies that promote sustainability.

Energy-efficient living not only benefits the environment but also saves you money in the long run. By adopting these practices, you can reduce your carbon footprint, lower your energy bills, and contribute to a more sustainable future for our planet.

It's a responsible and cost-effective way of life.

Chapter 8

Advocating for Green Living

Spreading the Word

In this chapter, we explore the power of advocacy and community engagement in promoting green living practices. It's not enough to embrace sustainable living in our personal lives; we must also advocate for change on a broader scale to create a more sustainable future.

Advocacy for a Greener World

Advocating for green living means actively working to raise awareness and inspire positive change in your community, region, and beyond. Here are some ways to become an effective advocate for green living:

1. Lead by Example

Your commitment to green living serves as a powerful example for others. People are more likely to embrace change when they see it successfully implemented in their communities.

2. Educate and Inform

Raise awareness about the importance of green living by sharing information and resources. Use social media, community workshops, or local events to educate others about the benefits of sustainable practices.

3. Support Sustainable Policies

Advocate for local and national policies that promote sustainability. This can include supporting renewable energy initiatives, advocating for public transportation, and encouraging green building standards.

4. Community Initiatives

Join or create community initiatives that focus on sustainable living. Participate in local cleanup events, community gardens, and green energy projects.

5. Collaborate with Organizations

Work with environmental organizations and groups dedicated to green living. Your efforts can be more impactful when you collaborate with like-minded individuals and organizations.

6. Green Living Challenges

Organize green living challenges in your community or workplace. Encourage people to make small, sustainable changes in their daily lives, and recognize and celebrate their efforts.

7. Sustainable Events

Support or organize eco-friendly events and fairs that showcase green products and practices. These events can provide a platform for local businesses and entrepreneurs who prioritize sustainability.

8. Advocacy Workshops

Host workshops on advocacy and sustainability. Equip people with the knowledge and tools to effectively advocate for green living practices and policies.

9. Encourage Sustainable Businesses

Support businesses that prioritize sustainable practices and let them know why you choose to do business with them. Your support can encourage other businesses to adopt eco-friendly measures.

10. Grassroots Campaigns

Engage in grassroots campaigns that address environmental issues in your community. Whether it's reducing plastic waste, conserving natural habitats, or promoting clean energy, grassroots efforts can make a significant impact.

11. Spread the Word

Use social media and traditional media to share your advocacy efforts and success stories. Social influence can be a powerful motivator for change.

12. Partner with Local Schools

Collaborate with local schools to introduce green living initiatives. These initiatives can include recycling programs, environmental education, and eco-friendly building designs.

13. Support Renewable Energy

Advocate for the use of renewable energy sources in your community. Push for the installation of solar panels, wind turbines, and other green energy solutions.

14. Encourage Sustainable Transportation

Promote sustainable transportation options like walking, cycling, and public transit. Advocate for bike lanes, pedestrian-friendly streets, and electric vehicle charging stations.

15. Be Persistent

Advocacy for a green living may face challenges and resistance. Be persistent and resilient in your efforts to effect positive change. Every small victory contributes to a greener world.

By advocating for green living, you become a catalyst for change, influencing your community and inspiring others to embrace sustainability. Your efforts can lead to a healthier environment, a more sustainable future, and a global shift towards responsible living.

Supporting Sustainable Initiatives

In a world increasingly aware of the environmental challenges we face, supporting sustainable initiatives is a vital step towards creating a more environmentally conscious and responsible society. Here's how you can contribute to and promote sustainable initiatives:

1. Invest in Sustainable Products

Support businesses that prioritize sustainability by purchasing their products. Look for eco-friendly labels and certifications when shopping for everyday items, from clothing to food.

2. Choose Renewable Energy

Opt for renewable energy sources, such as solar or wind power, for your home. Many utility providers offer green energy options, and investing in them helps expand the renewable energy market.

3. Support Local and Sustainable Agriculture

Purchase locally grown and sustainably produced food. Support farmers' markets, community-supported agriculture (CSA) programs, and restaurants that prioritize local and organic ingredients.

4. Reduce, Reuse, Recycle

Follow the three Rs: reduce your consumption, reuse items whenever possible, and recycle to divert waste from landfills. Encourage proper recycling in your community.

5. Sustainable Transportation

Use public transportation, carpool, bike, or walk when possible to reduce your carbon footprint. Support initiatives that improve public transit and promote electric vehicles.

6. Conservation Efforts

Contribute to conservation organizations and initiatives that protect natural habitats and biodiversity. You can also volunteer for local conservation efforts.

7. Eco-Friendly Gardening

Embrace sustainable gardening practices by using organic methods, conserving water, and creating pollinator-friendly landscapes. Support initiatives that promote green spaces.

8. Support Renewable Energy Policies

Advocate for policies that promote renewable energy at the local, state, and national levels. Join or support organizations that work towards clean energy and sustainability.

9. Sustainable Building and Design

Choose sustainable building materials and practices for construction and renovations. Support architects and builders who prioritize eco-friendly designs.

10. Environmental Education

Support programs and organizations that provide environmental education to schools and communities. Well-informed citizens are more likely to embrace sustainable living.

11. Circular Economy Initiatives

Promote the concept of a circular economy, where products are designed for durability, reuse, and recycling. Support businesses that adopt circular economy principles.

12. Sustainable Fashion

Choose clothing brands that prioritize sustainable and ethical practices. Encourage fashion companies to adopt eco-friendly materials and fair labor practices.

13. Renewable Energy Access

Advocate for increased access to renewable energy sources, particularly in communities that lack affordable and clean energy options.

14. Reduce Plastic Use

Support initiatives to reduce plastic waste, such as bans on single-use plastics, plastic cleanup efforts, and innovative alternatives to plastic products.

15. Green Financial Institutions

Choose financial institutions that invest in sustainable and environmentally responsible projects. Your banking and investment choices can have a significant impact.

16. Participate in Cleanups

Join or organize local cleanup events to remove litter and pollution from natural areas. These efforts help maintain clean and healthy environments.

17. Volunteer for Sustainability

Volunteer for organizations and initiatives that work towards sustainability. Whether it's tree planting, energy efficiency projects, or community gardens, your time and skills can make a difference.

18. Be a Conscious Consumer

Make thoughtful choices as a consumer. Consider the impact of your purchases on the environment and society, and support businesses that align with your values.

Supporting sustainable initiatives is not just an individual responsibility; it's a collective effort that can drive positive change on a global scale. By actively participating in and advocating for sustainability, you contribute to a greener and more sustainable future for all.

Engaging with Your Community

One of the most powerful ways to promote sustainability and green living is by actively engaging with your community. Local action can have a profound impact on creating a more environmentally conscious and responsible society. Here's how you can get involved and inspire positive change within your community:

1. Attend Community Meetings

Participate in local government meetings, town halls, and community gatherings to stay informed about environmental policies, projects, and issues. Express your support for sustainability initiatives and advocate for environmentally friendly policies.

2. Join Environmental Groups

Connect with local environmental organizations, such as conservation groups, climate action committees, or green living associations. Joining these groups allows you to network with like-minded individuals and participate in collective efforts to make your community more sustainable.

3. Volunteer for Clean-Up Events

Participate in community clean-up events focused on parks, rivers, and beaches. These events help maintain clean and healthy natural spaces and raise awareness about the importance of waste reduction.

4. Promote Sustainable Transportation

Advocate for and support initiatives that promote sustainable transportation options, such as bike lanes, pedestrian-friendly streets, and accessible public transit. Encourage carpooling and ride-sharing to reduce traffic congestion and emissions.

5. Green Community Spaces

Advocate for the creation and maintenance of green community spaces, such as urban gardens, parks, and natural reserves. These spaces enhance quality of life, improve air quality, and provide a place for community members to connect with nature.

6. Organize Eco-Friendly Workshops

Host workshops and information sessions on sustainable living practices, such as composting, recycling, energy conservation, and eco-friendly gardening. Educate your neighbors about practical ways to reduce their environmental footprint.

7. Support Local Farmers and Markets

Buy from local farmers' markets and support community-supported agriculture (CSA) programs. These initiatives help reduce food transportation miles, support local farmers, and provide access to fresh, locally-grown produce.

8. Create Sustainable Community Events

Plan and participate in sustainable community events that highlight green living, environmental protection, and conservation. These events can include eco-friendly fairs, sustainability expos, and green energy demonstrations.

9. Advocate for Renewable Energy

Encourage the adoption of renewable energy sources in your community. Support the installation of solar panels, wind turbines, and other green energy solutions.

Advocate for policies that make it easier for homeowners to go solar.

10. Participate in Local Decision-Making

Run for local government positions or participate in neighborhood committees that influence local decision-making. Having a voice in local politics can help shape policies that prioritize sustainability.

11. Support Eco-Friendly Businesses

Favor businesses in your community that prioritize eco-friendly practices and products. By supporting these businesses, you contribute to the growth of sustainable commerce and inspire others to follow suit.

12. Eco-Friendly Neighborhood Initiatives

Collaborate with your neighbors on sustainability initiatives, such as neighborhood tree planting, energy-efficient home upgrades, or communal gardens. These projects can strengthen the sense of community while promoting eco-conscious living.

13. Educate and Raise Awareness

Educate your community about environmental issues and sustainable living through presentations, community newsletters, or social media. The more people understand the importance of sustainability, the more likely they are to embrace it.

14. Support Sustainability in Schools

Engage with local schools to support environmental education programs and green initiatives. Encourage schools to integrate sustainability into their curricula and promote eco-friendly practices.

15. Build Relationships

Cultivate relationships with your neighbors and fellow community members. Building trust and camaraderie within your community makes it easier to rally support for sustainable causes.

By engaging with your community, you become a catalyst for positive change, helping to create a more sustainable and eco-conscious neighborhood. Together, you can inspire local action that contributes to a greener, healthier, and more environmentally responsible future.

Conclusion

Embarking on a green living journey is not merely a personal choice; it's a commitment to a better, more sustainable world. As you reflect on the information shared throughout this book, consider the strides you've made, the goals you've set, and the potential you have to inspire change in others.

Reflecting on Your Progress

Take a moment to acknowledge your achievements. Whether you've incorporated small changes in your daily routines or embarked on more significant sustainable endeavors, each step contributes to a larger, greener impact. Recognize your progress, and be proud of the difference you've made, no matter how small it may seem.

Setting Long-Term Goals

Green living is a journey without a final destination. Set long-term goals that continually challenge and motivate you. Whether it's reducing your carbon footprint, advocating for policy change, or further integrating sustainable practices into your life, these goals guide you toward a more environmentally conscious future.

Inspiring Others

Perhaps the most powerful aspect of your journey is your ability to inspire others. Sharing your experiences, knowledge, and passion for sustainability can ignite change in your community and beyond. Your influence has the potential to create a domino effect, encouraging others to join the movement towards a more sustainable world.

Your commitment to green living isn't just about the choices you make; it's about the impact you have on the world. Every decision you make in favor of sustainability ripples outward, influencing those around you and shaping a collective mindset for a healthier planet.

As you continue on this journey, remember that every effort counts. Every action, no matter how small, contributes to a larger, global shift toward sustainability. Your dedication to green living isn't just about the present; it's an investment in a future where our planet thrives, and future generations can enjoy its beauty.

Thank you for embracing the principles of green living and for being an advocate for a more sustainable, healthier, and happier world. Together, we can create a brighter future for all.